Contents

Introduction

The many new media which have come into being during the course of this century – from the Internet and computer software to TV cartoons – appear to fulfil many of the traditional roles of magazines and comics. Yet there are more magazines and comics available than ever before. Not only does each fresh development in the new media result in the launch of even more magazines and comics, but other media – from newspapers to TV programmes and from radio brodcasts to Websites – are becoming ever more like magazines. Meanwhile comics have evolved from light entertainment in newspapers, via entertainment for children, to encompass education, merchandising and sophisticated literary ideas.

Origins

People have always wanted information and entertainment that is fresh and up-to-date.

In humankind's earliest history, cave paintings and other early forms of art partly served this purpose by preserving records of important events and beliefs. Thousands of years later, news would be announced by messengers, such as the 'town crier'. As more people learned to read, written proclamations became more important, as they could be preserved and referred to again. This led, with the invention of printing, to the first newspapers and magazines.

The earliest magazines

Magazines were originally known as 'periodicals', a term that is still sometimes used today. They were given this name because they appeared at regular intervals, with a fixed period between each issue. This distinguished them from books and also from pamphlets. Magazines differ from newspapers in that they usually cover particular subjects or serve the interests of a specific **readership** and are published less often. Newspapers exist to provide a broad range of news to a wider section of the population, usually daily and never less often than weekly. That said, each newspaper has an individual style which makes it of greater interest to some readers than to others, and the availability of so many other sources of news, such as TV, has led newspapers to carry much more **feature** material.

From old gentleman to new lad

The past fifteen years has seen the launch of many new magazines for men, focusing on a range of traditional male interests – fashion and grooming, sport, adventure, sex and sexuality, careers and so on. They include *GQ*, *Esquire* (both launched as **spin-offs** from American magazines), *Arena*, *FHM* and *Loaded*. They have all found readerships within the adult male market by each having a subtle variation in emphasis.

For years, the industry had been doubtful whether such magazines could succeed. However, one of the first magazines ever launched had targeted men two-and-a-half centuries ago – *The Gentleman's Magazine*, first published in England in 1731! It was the first periodical to describe itself as a 'magazine'.

At that time there were no magazines for women. Why do you think this was the case?

This magazine, all fun and free gifts, had some very unlikely ancestors!

Today, there is literally no area of interest, from the most serious of thinking to the lightest of entertainment, that is not served by one or more magazines. However, it is worth remembering that in the early history of the medium, only the educated classes were literate and had the resources to produce and read magazines. This fact is underlined by the nature of the very earliest periodicals, which included:

• *Erbauliche Monaths-Unterredungen*, published in Germany from 1663 to 1668. The title means 'edifying monthly discussions'!
• *Philosophical Transactions*, launched in 1665 by the Royal Society of London.

During the 18th century, many periodicals were launched which still exist today, although their content has changed. These include *The Tatler* and *The Spectator*. Another periodical, *The Idler*, which was founded by the celebrated writer Samuel Johnson in 1758, has even been relaunched recently as a humorous magazine.

The coming of comics

Comics developed partly from the cartoons that appeared in periodicals during the 18th and 19th centuries, which satirized leading figures of the time, such as politicians. The English artist William Hogarth was probably the greatest caricaturist of his age and his work was very influential. The story-telling techniques used in illustrated books for children were also an important influence.

In 1895, the American Richard Fenton Outcault produced a **comic strip** called *Hogan's Alley* for the *New York Sunday World*. This was among the earliest examples of the form. Over the next 30 years, the formation of **newspaper syndicates** in the USA allowed smaller newspapers across the country to reproduce comic strips. These would often be placed in a special section of the paper, known as the 'funnies' – the forerunners of the first individual comics.

The satirical drawings of artists like William Hogarth (1697–1764) were among the forerunners of comics. Other artists who produced work like this during the 18th and 19th centuries included Thomas Rowlandson, George Cruikshank and James Gillray.

By the 1940s, comic strips had become quite sophisticated. The Spirit, by Will Eisner, ran for 650 episodes in an American Sunday newspaper.

Two different media

The overall market for both magazines and comics has continued to expand ever since their inception.

Similar, but ...

The two media do have certain similarities:

- they are published at regular intervals
- their printing and binding techniques are similar
- popular titles are available via newsagents
- more unusual titles are available from specialist outlets
- they rely heavily on reader loyalty for their continued success
- comparable titles compete with each other for readers.

However, as we have seen on pages 4–5, magazines and comics have very different ancestries, and even differ in their sources in the USA and the UK. American comics began as one very small piece of 'light entertainment' in a more 'serious' medium – the newspaper. The most immediate ancestors of British comics are the humorous and satirical 'comic papers' of the nineteenth century – one example, *Punch*, has survived well into the present day and has recently been relaunched (twice!).

Their non-literary origins have meant that comics have spent most of their history trying to establish their validity as a creative medium. This has been harder in the UK than in cultures such as the USA and Japan, where visual media have a longer tradition of development. Nevertheless, in these cultures, which have both produced comic strips for adults, even the most respected examples have a status that is perhaps closer to that of a well-crafted TV series than to literature.

Evolution and survival: Punch *shares the news-stands with its comic descendants.*

Magazines: media about media

Despite the proliferation of digital media, like the Internet and CD-ROMs, magazines are not easily replaceable. The profusion of titles covering such media as film, television, the Internet, photography, computers and software, music CDs, books and so on, confirms that magazines are an important, constantly updated reference source about other media.

This is true both of traditional media, like books, and of more recent developments, like recorded music, film and digital media of all kinds. As a general rule, whenever a new medium appears it is inevitable that one or more new magazines are launched to discuss it! Indeed, for readers in the magazine and news-trade business, there have even been magazines about magazines, such as *Magazine Week*.

Comic crossovers

Comics have an even longer history of media crossover, with one important difference: as most comics are vehicles for fiction, comic narrative can easily be recreated directly for other media. Batman, Superman, Flash Gordon and Wonder Woman are just a few of the most obvious comic characters who have also appeared in live-action and animated film, video, computer games and so on.

Today, this process works in all directions. Many films (like the *Star Trek* series) also have their stories realized as comics. Real people who are prominent in other media also appear in comics, like the rock band Kiss. The British adult comic *Viz* has taken this to amusing extremes by introducing real-life figures into the most unlikely contexts. For instance, pop singer Mick Hucknall has appeared in *Viz* as a football player and Jesus Christ has appeared in the guise of a rather irritating and fidgety schoolboy named Stan, whose parents tell him to 'Stop moving in a mysterious way!'

Media survivors

Given their ability to diversify, adapt and relate to other media, it seems unlikely that magazines and comics will ever be entirely replaced by other vehicles for entertainment and information. Furthermore, they:
- are entirely self-contained
- are inexpensive and readily available from thousands of outlets
- can be taken anywhere.

Or, to put it another way, imagine a medium that can carry thousands of words and images, is cheap enough to be disposable but durable enough to be preserved, requires no power, external equipment or special skills in its usage and can deliver information in an efficient, attractive way under virtually any circumstances. The most ordinary magazine or comic can do all of these things!

Manga!

Many Japanese comics are aimed at adults. They often have fantastic or science-fiction themes, frequently crossing over into video and film. Known as *manga*, they now have a strong following in the USA and Europe.

What do they cover?

Even the smallest minority interest can have its own magazine, as the readers of *The Haiku Quarterly* (look it up!) will no doubt testify.

How magazines are grouped

The publishing and advertising industries generally divide magazines into two types:
• trade magazines, which serve the interests of individual trades and professions
• consumer magazines, which are bought by members of the public either as entertainment or in support of their particular interests.

Many consumer magazines serve both of these purposes. For example, a magazine like *She*, targeted mainly at working mothers, combines practical articles on issues such as childcare and the workplace with more light-hearted columns and fashion coverage.

Within these categories there are many subdivisions. In the case of the trade press, the most obvious classification is by subject area, but there are magazines that serve the same profession at different levels. Examples of this include *Campaign* magazine, which serves the advertising profession, and *Marketing Week*, which serves the entire marketing sector of which advertising is one component. There are also magazines that serve a readership that exists within many different kinds of companies, regardless of the products or services those companies provide. For example, *Accountancy Age*, which is geared to the accountancy profession in general.

Both sides of the counter

Certain magazines, including the CD magazine *Gramophone* and the general science magazine *New Scientist*, function as both trade and consumer magazines. Such magazines are targeted at an intelligent readership with a special interest in the magazine's subject, and are sufficiently influential to affect the decisions made by both trade and consumer readers.

For example, *Gramophone* affects the choice of recordings bought by CD buyers, so record dealers follow the magazine closely to see which recordings they should stock.

New Scientist is read both by scientific professionals and by general readers who like to keep informed about scientific developments. This means that the professional readership follows the magazine very closely, because as well as providing information that is relevant to their work, the magazine also affects public opinion about scientific developments.

Two highly influential specialist magazines that serve both a trade and a consumer readership.

There is an accepted subdivision within consumer magazines between 'consumer' and 'specialist consumer' titles. The definitions of each type tend to shift depending on who is discussing the subject. For example, an **advertising agent** may consider the music magazine *Q* to be a general consumer title because of its large **circulation** (around 250,000) among a particular consumer group. However, as it is mainly devoted to music, *Q* may not be the ideal place to advertise, say, collectable ornaments, which would be more appropriate in a wide-ranging magazine such as a down-market Sunday newspaper colour supplement. In that respect, *Q* is arguably a specialist consumer title, but clearly less so than *Model Boats* magazine. Some specialist magazines may have a circulation as low as 1,000 and still be viable.

How comics are grouped

The categorization of comics is largely by targeted age-range, from pre-school to adult, and by narrative theme. Originally, the **syndicated** comic strips in newspapers would target that newspaper's readership, which would of course be adult. Typical among these were strips dealing with humorous views of domestic life, like the long-running syndicated American strip *Blondie and Dagwood* and their UK counterparts, such as *The Gambols* (appearing in the *Daily Express*, generally with their clothes on) and *George and Lynne* (appearing in the *Sun*, with Lynne's endless showering and topless sunbathing reflecting the newspaper's titillating approach).

Later – when the American press began to print a detachable 'funnies' section, which could be passed on to children in the household – comic strips that could be enjoyed at different levels by both children and adults began to appear. Charles M. Schultz's *Peanuts* strip – featuring the harassed Charlie

Batman: for all ages

DC Comics' Batman, created by the American Bob Kane in the 1930s, has become a major media icon, appealing to several successive generations of readers.

One unique result of Batman's enduring popularity is that Batman comics are now published not simply for children or adults but for young children, older children, teenagers, young adults and adults who are old enough to recall earlier stories about this character.

The two examples shown above are typical of the range.

Brown and his philosophical pet dog Snoopy – is among the most famous of these.

When comics began to be published in both the USA and the UK, they became readily identifiable by their intended age range and theme. For example, *Eagle* (mainly adventure stories and features for boys) and *Robin* (for very young children of both genders). Nowadays many comics, such as *2000 AD*, are targeted at both teenagers and adults.

How are they conceived?

How do new magazines and comics come to life?

New magazines

The launch of a magazine is generally motivated by one of two factors.

1 A good idea

Sometimes a publisher will want to produce a magazine that they feel will be important but which may not be self-funding. These are sometimes subsidized either privately or with money from a public body like the Arts Council of Great Britain.

2 A gap in the market

Usually, however, the concept is **market-led** – in other words, a publisher becomes aware that a gap exists in the general market for a particular type of magazine. This may be due to a new area of interest arising among a sufficiently large sector of the population. For example, the increased enthusiasm for football among a broader range of social groups led to the publication of new football magazines like *When Saturday Comes* and *Four Four Two*. The increased awareness of black culture has resulted in publications such as *The Source*.

Occasionally, a particular sector of the magazine business becomes unusually buoyant due to an upturn in the economy. This happened in the 1980s when a general increase in disposable income resulted in a dramatic increase in, for example, the market for women's magazines of the variety that emphasized home-making pursuits like cookery and crafts, together with a 'treat' element involving fashion, short fiction and anecdotal humour.

United we stand

One other variation on the market-led approach involves identifying areas of interest that overlap or are connected in some way in terms of consumer behaviour, then producing a magazine that reflects this.

Examples of this approach include:
• *Uncut* magazine, which covers a range of interlinked entertainment media such as film and CDs
• *SFX*, a science-fiction magazine which takes this subject as its central theme but covers film, video, audio, books, comics, games, etc.

Out to launch

Food and Travel is a relatively new magazine, launched by Fox Publishing, which capitalizes upon the obvious connection between these two areas of interest. When people take

Food and Travel *magazine*

holidays or short breaks, the opportunity to eat out and/or try different kinds of food is often a major factor in their enjoyment. The publisher researched this – using **focus groups**, studying existing travel and food magazines and assessing the overall potential of such a magazine – and concluded that:

• food, travel and lifestyle could be combined into one magazine

• no other magazines were serving the same market in this way

• food was undergoing an upsurge of interest, helped by such factors as 'personality chefs' on TV and the availability of a wider range of cooking ingredients than ever before

• other English-language markets, such as New Zealand, were able to sustain comparable magazines

• overseas **licensing** and distribution arrangements for the magazine were possible, which offered the possibility of special editions for other countries, thus adding to the circulation.

• it was possible to assemble a staff and contributors with the necessary expertise to produce such a magazine.

Based on these findings, the publisher was able to attract the necessary investment and advertising support to launch the magazine – so *Food and Travel* was born.

New comics

The launch process for new comics has changed significantly in recent years. Until the recent trend towards **cross-media ownership** and licensing, new launches were rare and publishers of 'traditional' comics like *The Beano* relied on their ongoing appeal, occasionally introducing new strips (or variations on old ones) but aiming to maintain their readership.

However, over the last 20 years, comics have increasingly relied on other media and

Teletubbies everywhere

It is no secret that the Teletubbies are a group of simple, colourful and childlike characters who feature in a series of TV programmes designed specifically for pre-school children.

The concept was initially controversial, as the notion of plonking very small children in front of the television seemed undesirable to some commentators. Of course, the creators of the show had simply realized that this happened anyway, but that there was very little programming for this age group – so they created some. The success of the programmes swiftly led to a range of related merchandising including 'must-have' toys, videos and a successful educational children's comic/magazine – a typical example of how new comics today are often derived from other media.

merchandising to provide a sustainable market. Recent examples in the UK have included *Postman Pat* and the *Teletubbies*, TV shows for children with **spin-off** products including comics and toys. This essentially removes the need for research, as the comics are targeted at existing markets. The BBC are particularly astute at creating comics to accompany their children's shows in this way. A similar process works well for their programme-related adult hobby magazines such as *BBC Gardener's World*.

Occasionally, the tail wags the dog. In the USA, Marvel Comics launched *Rom: Spaceknight* as a spin-off from a range of toys, but the comic was so well-conceived that it continued to be published for many years after the toys ceased production.

What you get: the words

The process of writing for magazines and comics has changed rather less than the system which causes the words to appear on the page.

Editors

Most magazines, other than the smallest, have a full-time editorial staff, some of whom may also write for the magazine. However, planning the magazine's content – and ensuring it actually appears – is central to their work. The editor of a comic may have similar responsibilities or, in the case of a one-story comic (usually American) such as those produced by DC Comics, Marvel Comics and so on, much of their time is devoted to supervision and, in particular, continuity.

Editorial responsibilities are divided in various ways by different magazines, but a typical list of personnel and their duties might be:

• *the editor*: oversees the general editorial policy of the magazine (thus being the person readers complain to) and usually has the final say about what does and does not appear; will often write an introductory item for each issue and may contribute other material as well; may commission work from writers, or may delegate this to ...

• *the deputy editor/assistant editor/features editor*: organizes contributions from **freelance** writers. A magazine may have one or more staff at this level and some define these editorial staff by the sections they are responsible for, such as 'fashion editor' or 'technology editor'

• *editorial assistant(s)*: provides support services, ranging from secretarial duties to handling day-to-day contact with contributors etc.

• *contributing editor(s)*: (a term more often used in US magazine publishing and mainly a courtesy title) supplies a large amount of the magazine's written content on a regular basis; usually freelance. They may never have edited anyone's work in their lives – least of all their own!

• *consultant editor(s)*: provides expert opinion on particular subject when required; usually freelance.

Editors? What editors?

Oddly enough, many of the skills originally demanded of magazine editors are now much less important. Copy-editing (also known as 'subbing', as the task was often carried out by staff called *sub-editors*) was for years an integral part of magazine publishing. This entailed checking the **copy** supplied by contributors for errors in spelling, grammar and punctuation, style of language and general accuracy – including ensuring that the material was the right length! Today, word processing

A typical modern magazine editorial department.

software can provide a word-count, as well as check spelling, words repeated in error and even grammar, and such editing can be done on-screen. The resulting text can then be converted by computer directly into the style of type that will appear in the finished magazine. This has made it possible to produce magazines with fewer staff, enabling small-circulation specialist magazines to be far more financially viable.

Writers

The role of the writer has largely remained unchanged, in terms of how they contribute to magazines, since the inception of the medium. Essentially, magazines need words, and writers provide them. Some larger magazines have full-time staff writers, much as newspapers have full-time reporters. However, the ways in which computer technology has eased the load of 'donkey work' on magazine staff means that a full-time magazine employee who writes for the publication is usually able to handle other editorial duties as well, such as overseeing a particular section of the magazine.

Much of the material that appears in magazines is provided by freelance writers. Some may be full-time writers, but others may have other jobs and write as a sideline. In the case of a magazine about a specific subject, a freelance contributor may hold a 'day job' relevant to the subject, while at the same time being a capable writer and so in an ideal position to write for the magazine.

One example is the hi-fi press, where the writers may also be audio engineers or technical consultants.

Comics and creativity

Modern comics generally operate in a similar way, except of course that artists as well as writers are contributors – and for some comic strips the same person will fill both roles.

Comics for younger children are usually produced fairly anonymously, with perhaps just a cheerful message from the editor on the opening page. However, comics for older children, teenagers and adults often build up an appreciation of individual writers and artists, crediting them for particular work and promoting particular strips on the strength of their reputations. This is particularly true of American super-hero comics, where *auteurs* like Alan Moore and Frank Miller have cult status.

Hi-Fi News *has only 3 full-time editorial staff, but draws on a pool of 30–40 freelance contributors to provide much of the magazine's content.*

What you get: the pictures

The illustrations in today's magazines and comics are created in a wide variety of ways.

How photographs appear in magazines

Photos are sourced for magazines in three ways:

1 Commissioned

Photos may be commissioned from a professional photographer, especially for magazines that rely a lot on stylish photography, like fashion magazines or those that use a lot of **reportage** shots (e.g. sports magazines). The photographer will often do regular work for a particular magazine. This helps to ensure some continuity of style, which is important in order to sustain the magazine's image. Also, magazine **deadlines** are often very tight, and reliable photographers whose work is distinctive and well-known to the magazine's designer, editor or picture editor are more likely to receive repeat commissions.

Some magazines – particularly those that specialize in covering celebrity lifestyles (like *Hello!*) – will accept **unsolicited** photographs if they are suitable for the magazine. This is also the case with many newspapers.

2 Researched

Photos may be researched. This is possible when there is a good chance of a suitable photograph of a given subject already having been taken. For example, a photograph of a well-known TV star can often be obtained from their agent or manager. There are also photo libraries which carry a large range of pictures of both general and specialized subjects – for example, the general library Popperfoto or the music-related specialist Redfern's. Shots can often be previewed in catalogue form (increasingly on digital media as well as print) and suitable pictures chosen. The publisher then pays an agreed fee to use the picture, which remains the property of the library.

3 Provided

Photos may be provided free of charge by a public relations company or by the equivalent department in a large company. Often the

The photos in this press pack may be very good – but who knows how many other publishers think so too?

quality of these photographs is acceptable and of course the publisher saves money by using them. However, if the magazine has a distinctive visual style, the photographs provided – which are often just straightforward pictures with no stylistic element – may not sit well with the rest of the magazine. Also, there is always a chance that another, competing, magazine will use exactly the same picture.

Photography and comics

Comics generally use drawn art rather than photographs. However, there are exceptions. Comics for young children that are based on TV programmes, like *Thomas the Tank Engine*, are often based around **stills** from the programmes. This can provide attractive visuals and also helps to link the comic and the programme in the mind of the reader. Adult comics occasionally use **photocollage** techniques with drawn art **overlays**, a technique used by Richard Corben in the French fantasy publication *Metal Hurlant*. Some strips aimed at teenagers will occasionally use the 'photostrip' technique. This involves shooting a sequence of black-and-white photos using real people, then laying **speech balloons** on top. One tabloid newspaper has used this method to illustrate medical and sexual problems for adults!

Graphics and illustrations

Other visual material is obtained from various sources.
• Cartoons are used in many magazines. These are provided as original drawings, usually in ink.
• Graphs and other technical illustrations may be commissioned from a specialist technical artist, although today such an artist would be more likely to use a computer graphics software package. A magazine's in-house design staff can easily produce some work of this kind – for example, **pie charts**.

• Original artwork may also be used in the magazine and often provides a pleasing contrast to other types of visual material.

Comics and art

In the case of comics, visual images are of course central to the medium. Traditionally, comic art is drawn in pencil on white art boards which are larger than the format of the comic itself to allow for increased detail (the final result is photographically reduced). The pencil art is then inked over and coloured, and lettering added to captions and speech balloons. This would usually involve one contributor for each step – pencilling, inking, colouring and lettering – but with the increasing recognition of individual talents in the comics' world, these tasks can now be the work of fewer individuals.

The importance of the visual element in comics demands different priorities than is the case with magazines.

What you get: the design

Magazines and comics are highly dependent on design, for both practical and artistic reasons. Reaching a balance between these two factors is far harder than it sounds!

On the one hand, a magazine should be:

• easy to read – over-complex design can be tiring for the reader
• properly structured – sections and features should be easy to find and identify
• free of visual errors, such as black type appearing on a dark grey background
• properly integrated – text, graphics and illustrations should 'hold together' in an intuitively 'right' way.

On the other hand, the publication must also be:
• easy to distinguish from its competitors
• easy to distinguish from its own previous issue – news-stand purchases of a newly-published issue are important and it must be obvious to a reader when a new issue is out
• visually interesting without being inappropriate to its subject.

Breaking the rules

Of course, there are problems with these generalizations. It may be that a new magazine, for example, is designed to look like its existing competitor. For instance, *Woman* and *Woman's Realm* are similar in appearance implying that *Womans Realm* could be tried as an alternative to *Woman*. This was very noticeable when several new TV listings magazines such as *TV Quick* were launched in the 1980s to compete with the long-established *Radio Times* and *TV Times*.

There are also very conservative areas of publishing where any overt design 'input' is regarded as frivolous and intrusive. For

The design of the music magazine NME *has evolved in line with its subject.*

example, when the *Literary Review* – a magazine about books – underwent a relatively subtle redesign, the editor said in his next opening editorial that he personally 'loved the old design, or lack of it'!

Redesign

Most magazines are redesigned occasionally. Publishers do this for various reasons. Often, changes in the content of the magazine will be best presented in a new way. The subject matter of the magazine will often be affected by fashion, and this will need to be reflected in the magazine's appearance. Also, most magazines wish to appear attentive and up-to-date in their thinking, and the visual impression they create is one way of achieving this.

Again, this is a difficult process. A fresh design may succeed in attracting new readers to pick up the magazine in newsagents. However, some browsers who pick up a redesigned magazine may also expect significant changes in the content. Should a redesign always go hand-in-hand with an editorial 'overhaul'? Or will this alienate existing readers? The biggest quandary of magazine design is how to attract new readers without alienating, or severely irritating, existing buyers.

Design tools

Much of the technical history of magazine design has been very close to that of the visual arts. In the early days, **hot-metal typesetting** and **engravings** were the main techniques used, and their limitations largely dictated how the final magazine would look. Today, **desktop publishing (DTP)** computer software such as Quark Xpress enables finished magazine pages to be assembled on-screen, incorporating text, graphics and illustrations. The results can then be output directly to the **film** that the printers use to make **plates** for printing.

Comic design

While the traditional design of children's comic strips has remained largely unchanged since their inception, the design of adult comics is constantly being readdressed.

This **DTP**-generated proof is a typical stage in modern magazine production.

For example, Alan Moore's *Watchmen* series borrowed the frame-by-frame narrative techniques used by film and TV. Other writers convey whole sections of narrative without using words at all. This is often used as a fairly **avant-garde** technique in Western comics, but Japanese *manga*, which have a very intense visual style, can often be 'read' purely from their sequence of images. This is very similar to very young children 'reading' comics by following the pictures before they have learned to recognize words, often making up their own story to fit the images.

Many other artists have added new ideas to comics in the past 30 years, particularly in the USA. In the 1970s, Jim Steranko borrowed whole ideas – including melting watches – from **surrealist** painting. Jack Kirby designed an entire comic which had to be read turned on its side. Several artists have used computer graphics and 'split page' techniques, where two distinct but connected stories run side by side, like sub-plots in a novel.

What you get: the ideas

The concepts behind magazines and comics have existed for centuries

I read, therefore I am

Magazine readers identify very strongly with their favourite magazines. There are many reasons for this:

• magazines usually have a particular, idealized reader in mind and produce a magazine for this reader

• this process is supported by research, of which readership surveys form an important part

• magazines are, by their nature, able to encompass many components of a type of lifestyle or area of interest and even to include columns that extend into other, related, areas. A reader should be able to look at a good magazine and see an idealized version of him- or herself looking back.

Comics and lifestyle

Children's comics reflect their readers' lifestyles mainly in fairly subtle, gentle ways. For example, the characters may have toys that are similar to those owned by the readers, and there is often a fantasy element involved. Comics with a direct link to merchandising or broadcasting, like the *Power Rangers* material of the early 1990s, have a more direct bearing on, for example, consumer behaviour. The group of comic characters created to promote the Burger King Kids' Club present a useful mix of ethnic backgrounds and degrees of ability – one character uses a wheelchair, for example.

iD *and identity*

iD magazine, launched in 1980, has refined the process of reader identity to an extraordinary degree. Generally described as being part of the style press, the fact that it has been published for 18 years shows that it has been successful in maintaining an up-to-date image among its primarily young, culturally-restless readership. Ironically, this youthful, cutting-edge magazine is now probably older than some of its readers!

iD *magazine has, appropriately enough, a very strong identity.*

THE FORWARD ISSUE NO.180

cover star *shalom* photographed by *carter smith october 1998*

£2.50 US$6.75

iD

fast forward

Teenage or adult comics often address lifestyle issues more directly, not only by incorporating more-or-less recognizable locations or products (for example, a character using a personal stereo on a train), but also by dealing with day-to-day personal, social and moral issues. The American publisher Marvel Comics excelled at this, creating heroes and heroines who had superhuman abilities but could also be divorced (The Wasp), have chronic feelings of guilt (Spider-Man), be an alcoholic (Iron Man) or be disabled (Box).

Magazines and lifestyle

Certain lifestyle magazines – for example, *Arena* for men and *Elle* for women – carry recommendations, or at least authoritative-sounding suggestions, about virtually every aspect of daily life. What to wear, where to buy it, what cosmetics to use, what to eat, where to eat it, what to cook it with, what to read and listen to, where to visit, how to have sex (and with whom) and much more is all bundled into these magazines. Of course, no one expects these lifestyle ideas to be followed slavishly, and often they fulfil a fantasy role in an idealized lifestyle, with the reader's complicity.

However, there are a few examples of the process working the other way. One company sold inexpensive perfumes by calling on possible customers in their workplaces. The company would add to their products' apparent value by buying advertising space for them in a well-known, lifestyle-influencing fashion magazine, for no other reason than to be able to show the advertisement to potential customers and say 'Look, this stuff is so good it's been advertised here!'

The readers of either of these magazines could be persuaded to buy a camera as a result of a magazine recommendation. However, they could probably not be persuaded to talk to each other!

Magazines – a way of life

Magazines can become a primary source of influence in the lives of their readers. The most obvious examples are magazines that review or describe products or services, providing recommendations from a source that the reader respects. For example, if the general leisure-and-entertainment-based consumer products magazine *Stuff for Men* recommends a particular camera, then one market for that product will have been reached. If the same camera is also recommended by the more serious and specialist *British Journal of Photography*, then a second market will also have been reached. Yet both readerships, while thoroughly influenced by the magazines they read, are quite different and would probably not get on if they met at a party!

What you get: the advertising

What kind of advertising do magazines and comics carry?

Much of the advertising in magazines is **display advertising**. As a general guide, advertisements of this type are designed to be noticed first and read second – if, indeed, they need to be read at all, as often the material consists of little more than a photograph and a logo. The magazine may also have a classified section, in which private individuals and smaller traders can place smaller ads which are usually charged for by the word or line. Semi-display advertisements are usually classified advertisements with a design or added visual element and are usually charged by the column centimetre.

Magazine advertising can also include loose and bound inserts – individual brochures or catalogues inserted between the pages. Similar material wrapped around the outside of a magazine is known as an outsert. There are also more controversial approaches to advertising, such as advertorials or advertising features, which can at first glance look like editorial recommendations. These are sometimes criticized as they may mislead readers, and guidelines exist as to their design – for example, editorial-like advertisements must generally be labelled 'advertisement'.

Why have ads?

Few magazines could survive on copy sales alone. Those that do are either subsidized, such as some literary magazines, or charge very high prices per copy, such as some art magazines. Most magazines rely on advertising revenue to keep their cover prices at an affordable level. Indeed, many magazines are launched purely because the publishers believe they will attract substantial amounts of advertising – the editorial content is almost an afterthought!

How ads get into magazines

The publisher has a sales team headed by an advertisement manager. Their job is to attract and maintain advertisers by persuading them that the magazine's particular combination of circulation, **environment**, **rates** and readership profile makes it a good advertising medium for their product (or, in the case of advertising agencies, their client's product). The publisher will usually provide a media pack – a folder of facts and figures about the magazine, together with advertisement rates.

Just say no!

Advertising is such a fundamental part of most magazines that it can have a profound effect on the publication's overall identity. One well-known music magazine once turned down a lucrative advertising contract for an anti-drugs campaign. Most of the campaign targeted teenagers and young adults. However, this particular magazine had a slightly older adult readership. When this was pointed out, the advertising agency agreed, but felt that readers of this particular magazine were more likely than average to frequent places where dangerous drugs were used! The publisher disagreed and, quietly horrified, politely declined to carry the advertising.

Comics and advertising

Comics have always depended more on copy sales than advertising for their revenue, and their advertising element has never been large. Today, most advertising in UK children's comics relates to merchandising **tie-ins**. Examples include toys, games and events relating to the characters – from *Thomas the Tank Engine* play mats to a touring performance show featuring the *Power Rangers*. Occasionally such items as food products aimed at children may also be included. However, in American comics, ads aimed at children for products like mail-order toys were once common. Another example – targeting young capitalists – encouraged readers to sell a news magazine called *Grit* to friends and neighbours. This kind of advertising is now much less widespread.

This Milkybar ad is typical of the largely harmless advertising that can be found in UK comics today.

DID YOU KNOW?•FACTS & FIGURES•INDUSTRY

Industry research: death by acronyms

THE ADVERTISING PROCESS IS ALSO SUSTAINED BY A GREAT DEAL OF RESEARCH, INVOLVING AN ALARMING NUMBER OF CONFUSING INITIALS:

TGI (TARGET GROUP INDEX) PRODUCES STATISTICS ABOUT THE POPULATION AND RELATES THEM TO MEDIA USAGE

BRAD (BRITISH RATE AND DATA) IS A BOOK LISTING ADVERTISING RATES FOR ALL UK MEDIA

THE ABC (AUDIT BUREAU OF CIRCULATIONS) PRODUCES OFFICIAL, **AUDITED** CIRCULATION FIGURES.

MANY OTHER RESEARCH TOOLS AND ORGANIZATIONS SERVE THIS SECTOR.

Publishing adspeak – a user's guide

How to avoid those embarrassing gaffes!

• 'Advertisement' is correct, 'ad' is colloquial and cool, 'advert' is neither!

• *Advertising* managers work for companies who advertise in publications. *Advertisement* managers work for magazines, where they sell advertising to advertising managers.

• 'Perfect bound' is a technique whereby thick magazines are bound like a paperback book, by gluing along one edge. It is *not* a statement about the quality of the binding!

Sales and promotion

Being able to publish a magazine with satisfactory editorial content and a healthy amount of paid advertising is pointless if no one actually wants to buy the magazine.

There are two main channels through which magazines are sold – by postal subscription and via retail outlets.

Subscribe now!

Magazine subscribers elect to pay in advance for a number of magazines – usually a year's worth – which are then sent by post. This is the ideal way for a publisher to sell magazines, as they receive all the payment 'up front'. This means that most magazines are always trying to attract new subscribers and will often offer incentives – for example, a free gift to new subscribers, a reduction in cost in comparison with the news-stand price, special 'subscribers-only' offers and so on.

UK children's comics are much more likely to be browsed through or reserved at newsagents' shops as, at least from the adult viewpoint, they are often a more casual

Splat!

The sound of a favourite magazine landing on the doormat is always welcome. However, many publishers simply mail subscription copies in a transparent polythene bag and do not attempt to capitalize on the goodwill that has persuaded a reader to pay in advance for a year's supply of magazines.

By contrast, Future Publishing, who produce a range of magazines catering for many areas from computing to needlework, make good use of this opportunity. Their standard subscription envelope features:

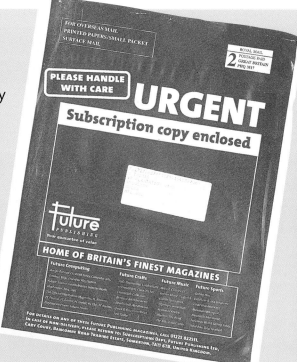

- large messages about careful handling and urgency, reinforcing customer care
- the company's logo and slogan
- a detailed list of the other magazines produced by the same publisher, gently making the recipient aware of other titles of interest
- a return address and contact phone numbers for any queries.

The envelope itself is made of durable polythene with a black interior, to discourage theft in transit – the magazine remains unidentifiable until the package is opened.

An alternative idea used by some publishers is to sell the wrapper as advertising space.

purchase. Free gifts are often an incentive. Publishers of these comics are also more likely to withdraw titles at short notice – for example, if a tied-in TV show is cancelled. Encouraging and then refunding subscriptions under these circumstances makes little economic sense, so the facility is not usually well-promoted but may exist as an option.

Browsing and buying

Retail sales of magazines and comics are made through general newsagents and specialist outlets. For example, a magazine about wine may also be sold in wine shops and there are shops that sell only comics, although these are mainly geared to adult collectors.

While subscribers are ideal buyers, many readers prefer to be able to flick through a magazine, perhaps comparing it with competing titles, before deciding whether or not to buy it. The magazines are usually supplied to the shops by a distributor or wholesaler, who will handle them in bulk. Some large companies, such as WH Smith, are both retail chains and wholesalers, supplying their own and other shops. Some regular readers prefer to have their chosen magazine reserved by a newsagent, who can also order specialist titles. This means that the reader does not have to pay for a full year in advance and can cancel or change to another magazine at any time. While this may, over a year, be more expensive than a subscription, some foreign magazines (e.g. those from the USA) will cost less when bought like this, as they can be imported in bulk and sold only at the cover price, avoiding the postage costs for an overseas subscription.

Many techniques, such as free gifts or special displays can be used to encourage retail purchase of magazines and comics.

A teenage magazine with a free gift attached.

With compliments ...

The exceptions to these methods are certain trade magazines which are supplied via a controlled circulation. This means that the publisher identifies a list of suitable recipients and sends them each issue of the magazine free of charge. This is usually closely tied to the advertising in the magazine. For example, a trade magazine devoted to industrial waste management might identify, say, the top 10,000 companies who use waste disposal equipment. The executive responsible for buying this equipment would be sent this magazine every month, free of charge. The magazine's advertisers would then be assured of reaching the type of reader who might buy their products.

Distribution

The distribution of magazines and comics is a highly pressurized process.

The schedule for assembling a magazine's editorial and advertising content, or a comic's art and text, and completing its design, production and printing leads directly into a second schedule. This distribution schedule involves the delivery of copies (usually directly from the printer) to wholesalers and subscription **fulfilment** companies, and ends with the date the magazine is due to go on sale.

Tomorrow won't do!

Unlike many other products, magazines and comics absolutely must be available on the pre-arranged date. There are several reasons for this:

• Magazines and comics are bought on the assumption that their content covers a specific period. If this appears to change, readers will be disappointed.

• Advertisers often buy space in a magazine or comic with

a view to covering an exact period of time with their advertising. This may be because their campaign is appearing in several media and the advertiser wants to judge their effectiveness, in which case any advertising that appears too late or too soon will confuse the results. Their advertising may also be tied in with the launch of a new product – often the case with toy advertising in comics – or with a particular event such as an exhibition or TV show, making their advertising **date-sensitive**.

• Because there are so many people and companies involved in the production of magazines and comics, any delay at any stage has a knock-on effect on the next stage and on any other projects that are being worked on. For example, a printer will have allocated a particular period of time for printing a magazine or comic. If it arrives late at the factory, then the printing press will be idle while the printer waits for the work to turn up. A distributor will be expecting to deliver the magazines/comics on a certain date. If they do not arrive, then the delivery must go ahead without that particular title.

• Delays are embarrassing for the publisher, as they send a negative message to readers, advertisers and the rest of the magazine industry.

This advertiser would be extremely annoyed to find that the magazine in which they advertised didn't reach the news-stands until the day after the event.

Post-haste

The supply of magazines and comics on subscription is equally sensitive. Postal strikes, bad weather and even fulfilment companies suddenly going bankrupt (it happens!) can leave a pile of magazines or comics in a warehouse with no chance of reaching their readers on time. Late arrival – or non-arrival – of subscription copies is very damaging to customer relations.

Comics and faith

Children's comics are subject to most of the same demands in terms of supply as magazines, except that, because many of them are weekly and have a very young readership with *absolute* expectations, customer goodwill is all-important. Adult comics are produced to the same rigorous schedules in terms of production and distribution. However, they are often bought weeks or months after publication – except special collectors' editions, which are often reserved in advance.

The magazine as time machine

Many UK comics are weekly, and most monthly comics are US imports, which affects their UK on-sale date. But have you ever wondered why so many monthly magazines appear weeks before the dates shown on their covers?

There are many reasons. One is competition. Publishers have always reasoned that catching the 'floating reader', interested in a given subject but uncommitted to any specific magazine, is important – after all, they may become permanent. One way of doing this is to get your magazine in front of them before the others. So, if the October issue of *What Sock?* appears on the first Thursday in October, *Sock User* may decide to publish their October issue on the last Thursday in September. Then *Your Sock* decides to go one better and publish halfway through September, and so on.

One other reason dates from earlier this century, when the international delivery of subscription copies would often take weeks. Some magazines dated their issues ahead in the hope that their one reader in Lapland would be happier to receive an issue in February dated January than one dated December. In fact, of course, it had been printed in November anyway!

Time is an illusion …

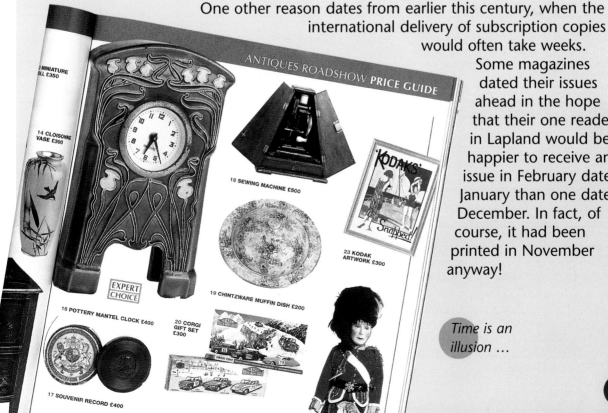

ANTIQUES ROADSHOW PRICE GUIDE

MINIATURE DOLL £350

14 CLOISONNE VASE £300

18 SEWING MACHINE £500

'KODAKS' Snapped!

23 KODAK ARTWORK £300

EXPERT CHOICE

19 CHINTZWARE MUFFIN DISH £200

16 POTTERY MANTEL CLOCK £400

20 CORGI GIFT SET £300

17 SOUVENIR RECORD £400

21 SILVER NUTCRAS...

Magazines, comics, ethics

As media, magazines and comics have always been a moral and ethical battleground and have often been subject to **censorship**.

The reasons for this have as much to do with the practicalities of their production as the points of view they may represent. A magazine or comic is easy to produce and circulate, and cheap to buy, yet it can be preserved and/or passed on to many other readers. The format admits all kinds of material – text, photographs, graphics, cartoons – and the frequency of publication allows debate between contributors in successive magazine issues.

These debates are often reinforced by readers who contribute to the letters pages (and who will often carry on their own exchanges of views, if permitted to do so by the editor).

Magazines and comics are easily launched, closed, bought up, suspended, sold or relocated. This makes them much less vulnerable to external influences than, say, broadcasting companies, which require massive budgets, a large number of staff and permanent facilities. A magazine is a moving target and the idea behind it will often survive several changes of publisher, editor, format and, to an extent, content.

Pros and cons

The adaptable nature of magazines and comics means that they can be used to express any viewpoint in a way that can be both far-reaching and influential. Often this is manifest in a very straightforward and uncontroversial way. For example, *The Railway Magazine*, founded in 1897 and still going strong, simply contends that railways are interesting. This notion is hardly likely to attract adverse attention even from the anti-pollution lobby, who might be more likely to direct their objections to a magazine like *Redline*, which encourages interest in fast cars.

However, other magazines are explicitly geared to covering controversial issues – some sincerely and others simply to sell more copies. Magazines such as *New Internationalist* deal directly with social, political and economic issues, aiming to draw attention to global inequality, poverty and oppression. Supporters of the regimes criticized in such activist magazines often

No. 307 / NOVEMBER 1998

THE
NI
NEW INTERNATIONALIST

PRICE: UK £2.50 AUS. $5.90 AOTEAROA/NZ $5.90 CANADA/US $4.50 ● THE PEOPLE, THE IDEAS, THE ACTION IN THE FIGHT FOR WORLD DEVELOPMENT

Red and Green

Eco-socialism
comes of age

◆ **Greenprint for the future**

◆ **Mama Afrika**

◆ **Reasons to be fearful**

This magazine is devoted to ethical issues on a global scale.

target them for reprisals. These can range from letters to the editor to firebombing their premises.

At the other extreme are magazines like *Bizarre*, which deal in sensational themes often involving sex or the occult. Between the two lie a whole range of philosophies and **ideological** stances, monitored by various regulatory bodies. The **Press Council** is responsible for 'policing' the ethics of editorial material and the **Advertising Standards Authority** deals with complaints about advertisements.

An ethical minefield

Even entirely sensible, down-to-earth magazines, covering mainstream subjects, are obliged to constantly monitor their own ethical position. Often the most unexpected factors create an ethical minefield for the publisher. For instance, one music magazine published an article that was highly critical of the state subsidy of music in a particular country. The argument was taken up by that country's national press which, being published daily, was able to escalate the debate to artificially high proportions far beyond the article's original intention.

Less seriously, however ...

Sometimes the ethical issues surrounding magazines and comics can assume an entertaining dimension. *Viz*, a rather rude humorous magazine in comic strip format for adults, described itself as a 'comic'. One major retailer objected, reasoning that the 'comic' category was only appropriate for publications for children. *Viz* allegedly responded by describing their publication as a 'bomic'.

An example of the hard-hitting work of Harvey Kurtzman. This kind of thing never happens in Fireman Sam!

Comics: not always funny

The humble comic has been subject to a high level of ethical debate for half a century. One early example was the work of the American comics artist Harvey Kurtzman, whose work showed the horrors of war, rather than presenting it as entertaiment.

The publisher was able to bypass censorship laws as no photographs were used. Eventually, a body was formed in the USA called the Comics Code Authority, which regulated the level of violence depicted in the medium. More recently this has been less of an issue and comics produced for adults which may contain material unsuitable for children are generally marked as such.

The magazine as chameleon, the comic as literature

Magazines and comics are still evolving – often in surprising ways.

The magazine format

The structure of the magazine 'package' has proved to be one of the strongest and most versatile in the media landscape. Both existing and new media are increasingly adopting the magazine format as a means of conveying information.

Here are a few examples:
• Television has described certain programmes as having a 'magazine format' for several decades. One such programme, now known to several generations of viewers, is the popular general knowledge programme for children, *Blue Peter*.
• Talk radio often adopts a magazine format for programmes aimed at particular interest groups, such as BBC Radio 4's arts and culture programme *The Saturday Review*.
• Newspapers, finding their primary role as news media being usurped by TV and other services, are increasingly looking like magazines. Their front pages may be news-led, but they are increasingly filled with non-news items, such as non-date-sensitive feature coverage. The Saturday *Guardian* is a sophisticated example of this. A recent issue comprised a

Many internet sites have a magazine-like structure, with a contents page leading to news features etc.

newspaper, a sports newspaper, a weekly review, a jobs and finance section, an arts listings magazine, a general features magazine, a fashion magazine and 'The Editor' presenting a non-date-sensitive 'digest' of news, features and opinion from a variety of sources (including foreign-language publications translated into English) for people who are unable to keep up with them directly! Perhaps this is because they have to spend the whole week reading the Saturday *Guardian*!

Comics and culture

Like popular music, comics are now seen as having acquired a degree of cultural maturity. This has as much to do with the changing perceptions of readers who have grown up with the medium and who are now in a position to 'formalize' their understanding of it. For example, the strip *Lord Snooty and his Pals*,

Of course it's a magazine ...

The ability of the magazine format to cross over into media other than conventional print is not a recent discovery. The idea predates both the CD format and the widespread use of the Internet, particularly in the field of the visual arts.

Engaged is an art magazine with each issue in a different medium. The first was published on a tee-shirt, the second on a poster, the third as a CD-ROM and the fourth as a ring-pull can containing texts, print artworks and small sculptural objects (including some string!)

which ran for many years in *The Beano*, can now be analysed as a model of how different personality types can interact. The mixture of characters encompasses vanity (Liz), brashness (Scrapper), mischief (Snitch and Snatch) leadership (Snooty) and so on, relying on well-defined protagonists just as classic literary authors such as Charles Dickens did. This process is much more overt in adult comics, which are often structured in a novel-like way and published or republished as 'graphic novels' – for example, Todd Macfarlane's *Spawn*.

Digital days

The advent of digital media has had a profound effect on the concept of the magazine. Many music and computer magazines now have a cover-mounted CD or CD-ROM that is an integral part of the magazine. Typical among these are computer magazines such as *Ultimate PC*, which covermounts samples of PC games software which are discussed in the magazine. There are a few magazines that have even reversed

this order of priority. For example, CD-ROM-only titles are sometimes sold among the magazines on news-stands, mounted on magazine-sized cards for display purposes.

Typical Internet sites have always been modelled, perhaps not even consciously, on magazines. Increasingly, the people who put these sites together are describing themselves as 'Internet publishers'. Many print magazines now have a Web site which provides additional material.

The future

It seems likely, therefore, that the magazine will always be with us. What is changing, however, is the idea that a magazine can only be a printed artefact between two covers. As new media continue to develop and traditional media are re-evaluated, it seems probable that, whatever happens, there'll be magazines published using that medium – and probably several more about it! Comics, in the meantime, are well on the way to becoming a fully-fledged literary form.

Key dates

1663	Launch of the first identifiable periodical, *Erbauliche Monaths-Unterredungen*, in Germany.
1731	Launch of *The Gentleman's Magazine*, one of the earliest magazines to be published in the UK.
1758	*The Idler* magazine founded in the UK by Samuel Johnson.
1830	Launch of *Godey's Lady's Book* – one of the first influential magazines for women.
1842	Launch of the *Illustrated London News*, one of the first modern illustrated magazines.
1895	*Hogan's Alley*, one of the earliest newspaper comic strips, starts to appear in the New York *Sunday World*.
1900	Photography has by now largely replaced art in illustrated magazines.
1922	Launch in the USA of *Readers' Digest*, a magazine anthology of material from other sources. It sells so many copies that it does not accept advertising until 1955.
1923	The profusion of magazines on all subjects is acknowledged by writer Compton Mackenzie, who, on launching the music magazine *Gramophone*, wryly apologizes to the public for starting yet another one.
1923-33	Launch of international news magazines such as *Time* and *Newsweek*.
1938	First issue of *Action Comics* published. Its lead character, Superman, becomes one of the most iconic figures in popular culture.
1939	First appearance of Batman in US comic strips. The character's creator, Bob Kane, remains involved with the many different interpretations of the character until his death in 1998. World War II begins; paper rationing affects the publication of magazines and comics, but many survive by reducing issue sizes or frequency of publication.
1950	The *Eagle* comic for boys launched in the UK by Marcus Morris. It featured strips providing a more 'wholesome' alternative to imported American comics, which Morris described as 'deplorable'.
1957	*GQ* magazine launched in the USA. The publishing industry in general catches up with the idea of men's style magazines 25 years later.
1977	Creation of the Apple II computer, which has a colour display and keyboard – the precursor of …
1984	… the Apple Mac, an affordable computer with sophisticated graphic capabilities, allowing the development of desktop publishing.
1993	Launch of *Wired* magazine, covering computer technology and the Internet.
1997	The term 'Internet Publisher' becomes commonplace, denoting people who produce magazine-like information packages on Web sites.

Glossary

advertising agent a company that creates and places advertising for a client

Advertising Standards Authority the 'watchdog' organization of the advertising industry, which exists to ensure that all advertising is 'legal, decent, truthful and honest'

audited checked by independent accountants

auteurs (from the French word for author) a person who creates and/or controls most or all the ideas in a work of art

avant-garde the most innovative area of an art form

censorship the restriction of information, which may either be beneficial (e.g. preventing children from witnessing media violence) or repressive (e.g. stifling certain political or religious views)

circulation the actual number of copies of a publication that are sold

comic strip originally a short sequence of drawings forming a story, printed in a newspaper. Named because of its horizontal shape. The term is sometimes used in reference to comics in general

copy editorial or advertising matter

cross-media ownership when one company owns, say, a publishing company and a broadcasting network – occasionally controversial, as this could theoretically lead to too much control of the media in general being in the hands of too few companies

date-sensitive useful only until a certain date, e.g. promotional activity for a sports event

deadlines dates by which certain tasks, such as the submission of copy, must be completed

desktop publishing (DTP) producing a publication using computer facilities such as word processing and design software – DTP often allows much of the work to be done at one desk

engravings pictures created by cutting lines into a hard surface, from which prints can be made

environment the content and design of material adjacent to an advertisement

feature a (usually fairly long) detailed item in a magazine or newspaper which focuses on a particular subject or theme

film photographic material used in the printing process (e.g. for making printing plates)

focus group a group of consumers who are gathered together for discussions, as an aid to market research

freelance an employee who works independently for more than one company

fulfilment the provision of a routine service, such as magazine subscriptions

hot-metal typesetting type for printing made by pouring molten metal into moulds

ideological relating to a particular set of ideas held by an individual or group

licensing an agreement that allows one company to use and/or sell a brand or product created by another company

market-led a business initiative led by proven market demand

merchandising using branded goods to sell or promote another product or service

newspaper syndicate a group of newspapers that share their content and which may also have other business links

overlays pieces of artwork produced on transparent material which allows other material to show through

photocollage the assembly of various pieces of photographic material to produce one final image

plates the surfaces (usually metal) used in printing

Press Council a 'watchdog' body that monitors the editorial standards of the press

rates in publishing this usually refers to advertising charges

readership the total number of people who read a publication – often higher than circulation, as copies can be passed on to other readers

reportage the presentation of actual events in a publication

sourced obtained from

speech balloons used in comics, these are small shapes containing dialogue, with a pointer indicating the speaker

spin-offs products or services derived from - or which began as part of – other products or services

stills single images from a film or video

surrealist a style of art influenced by dreams and the subconscious

syndicated paid for jointly by several organizations

tie-ins additional products or services based on another concept or medium (e.g. a book about the making of a popular film)

unsolicited provided without being asked for

Index